This is a *codex:*

The codex maps the letters a, b, c, ...
onto the letters c, t, s, ...

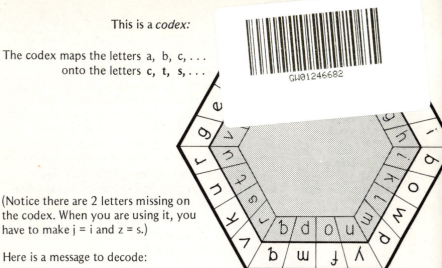

(Notice there are 2 letters missing on the codex. When you are using it, you have to make j = i and z = s.)

Here is a message to decode:

Pcoa lfrv fey sfhax.

> If you trace and cut out the inner hexagon of letters, you could fit it back in six ways.
>
> So you can get six different codes from a codex.

Each of the six messages below uses a different one of the six codes that you can get from the codex. So to decode them you will have to decide which code is being used in each case.

No clues given! But you may find it useful to know that the messages are about a Sherlock Holmes story called 'The Dancing Men'.

1. C pcy scwwah Sfycy Hflwa evfua kufvbak ctfru Kiavwfso Ifwpak
2. Egy ef sqyty tsecvyt nbt wbuuyp 'Sqy Pbgwvgm Ryg'.
3. Ab mhaf fmoyr mhcyc kcyc tavc xolcl icffgscf mghm dooncl danc yokf ot igbxabs icb.
4. Qnp uva ogg wlg rvaucax hga na dvxg wlbgg.
5. Tpbv hkl pacb ibdkibi xpbeb eys qbeeawbe hkl qywpx xgh xpb iavdyvw qbv.
6. Fid drvp'av ctd vynp, ycq tc syuv ktia pti myc avyq rto Nrvaxtme Rtxlvn maymevq drv mtqv.

1

The dancing men

This story tells how Sherlock Holmes had a visit from a Mr. Hilton Cubitt who brought with him the 'dancing men' which you can see on p. 3. Cubitt said that his wife, Elsie, was an American lady whom he had married only a year back. He had promised never to inquire into her past life which, she said, she wanted to forget. But now these messages had begun to appear, chalked on the walls of their country house, or pencilled on scraps of paper left in their garden. Elsie was obviously frightened by them, but still she told her husband nothing.

Can you make out what the dancing men are saying? (It's not easy, and if you want a clue, there is one at the bottom of this page.)

On pp. 4-6 you can read how Sherlock Holmes decoded the messages.

Clue to the Dancing Men: The first message contains the name Abe Slaney.

A note about uni-composite numbers. (You won't need this until you want to use the coding method on page 16).
How many pairs of numbers can you find that multiply together to make 12? 13? 14?
Quite a few for 12: $12 = 1 \times 12 = 2 \times 6 = 3 \times 4$
Only one pair for 13: $13 = 1 \times 13$
And just two pairs for 14: $14 = 1 \times 14 = 2 \times 7$
So 13 is called a *prime number*, which means that it has got only one pair of factors — itself and 1.
And 12 is called a *composite number*, which means that it has got several pairs of factors. Well, more than one pair at least.
Now, numbers like 14, which have got just one pair of factors besides itself and 1, we are going to call *uni-composite*.
Here's a couple of checks to make sure you understand this:

1. For the numbers between 20 and 30:   23 and 29 are *prime*
                                            24 and 28 are *composite*
                                            21, 22, 25, 26 and 27 are *uni-composite*

   Do you see why?

2. Sort out the numbers between 1 and 20 in the same way.
   You should find seven uni-composite numbers. If they add up to 66, you've probably picked the right ones!

1 Holmes held up the paper so that the sunlight shone full upon it. It was a page torn from a notebook. The markings were done in pencil, and ran in this way:

🕺🕺🕺🕺🕺🕺🕺🕺🕺🕺🕺

Holmes examined it for some time, and then, folding it carefully up, he placed it in his pocket-book.

2 the lawn in full view of the front windows. I took an exact copy, and here it is." He unfolded a paper and laid it upon the table. Here is a copy of the hieroglyphics:

🕺🕺🕺🕺🕺🕺🕺

"Excellent!" said Holmes. "Excellent! Pray continue."

3 but two mornings later a fresh inscription had appeared. I have a copy of it here ":

🕺🕺🕺 🕺🕺🕺

Holmes rubbed his hands and chuckled with delight. "Our material is rapidly accumulating," said he.

4 Again he produced a paper. The new dance was in this form:

🕺🕺🕺🕺

5 sundial. He enclosed a copy of it, which is here reproduced:

🕺🕺🕺🕺🕺🕺 🕺🕺🕺🕺 🕺🕺🕺 🕺🕺🕺

Holmes bent over this grotesque frieze for some minutes and then suddenly sprang to his feet with an exclamation of surprise and dismay. His face was haggard with anxiety.

"We have let this affair go far enough," said he. "Is there a train to North Walsham to-night?"

From Sir Arthur Conan Doyle, *The Return of Sherlock Holmes*. Baskervilles Investments Limited and Jonathan Cape Limited/John Murray (Publishers) Limited.

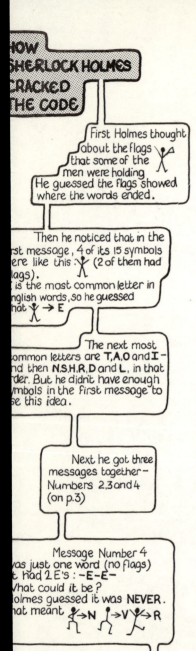

"Having once recognized, however, that the symbols stood for letters, and having applied the rules which guide us in all forms of secret writings, the solution was easy enough. The first message submitted to me was so short that it was impossible for me to do more than to say with some confidence that the symbol stood for E. As you are aware, E is the most common letter in the English alphabet and it predominates to so marked an extent that even in a short sentence one would expect to find it most often. Out of fifteen symbols in the first message four were the same, so it was reasonable to set this down as E. It is true that in some cases the figure was bearing a flag, and in some cases not, but it was probable from the way in which the flags were distributed that they were used to break the sentence up into words. I accepted this as an hypothesis, and noted that E was represented by

" But now came the real difficulty of the inquiry. The order of the English letters after E is by no means well-marked, and any preponderance which may be shown in an average of a printed sheet may be reversed in a single short sentence. Speaking roughly, T, A, O, I, N, S, H, R, D, and L are the numerical order in which letters occur; but T, A, O, and I are very nearly abreast of each other, and it would be an endless task to try each combination until a meaning was arrived at. I, therefore, waited for fresh material. In my second interview with Mr. Hilton Cubitt he was able to give me two other short sentences and one message, which appeared—since there was no flag—to be a single word. Here are the symbols. Now, in the single word I have already got the two E's coming second and fourth in a word of five letters. It might be 'sever,' or 'lever,' or 'never.' There can be no question that the latter as a reply to an appeal is far the most probable, and the circumstances pointed to its being a reply written by the lady. Accepting it as correct, we are now able to say that the symbols stand respectively for N, V, and R.

" Even now I was in considerable difficulty, but a happy thought put me in possession of several other letters. It occurred to me that if these appeals came, as I expected, from someone who had been intimate with the lady in her early life, a combination which contained two E's with three letters between might very well stand for the name 'ELSIE.' On examination I found that such a combination formed the termination of the message which was three times repeated. It was certainly some appeal to 'Elsie.' In this way I had got my L, S, and I. But what appeal could it be? There were only four letters in the word which preceded 'Elsie,' and it ended in E. Surely the word must be 'COME.' I tried all other four letters ending in E, but could find none to fit the case. So now I was in possession of C, O, and M, and I was in a position to attack the first message once more, dividing it into words and putting dots for each symbol which was still unknown. So treated it worked out in this fashion:

. M . ERE .. E SL . NE .

"Now, the first letter can only be A, which is a most useful discovery, since it occurs no fewer than three times in this short sentence, and the H is also apparent in the second word. Now it becomes:

AM HERE A . E SLANE .

Or, filling in the obvious vacancies in the name:

AM HERE A . E SLANEY.

I had so many letters now that I could proceed with considerable confidence to the second message, which worked out in this fashion:

A . ELRI . ES.

Here I could only make sense by putting T and G for the missing letters, and supposing that the name was that of some house or inn at which the writer was staying."

Inspector Martin and I had listened with the utmost interest to the full and clear account of how my friend had produced results which had led to so complete a command over our difficulties.

"What did you do then, sir?" asked the Inspector.

"I had every reason to suppose that this Abe Slaney was an American, since Abe is an American contraction, and since a letter from America had been the starting-point of all the trouble. I had also every cause to think that there was some criminal secret in the matter. The lady's allusions to her past and her refusal to take her

---

Message Number 3 ended with a word: E---E, Holmes thought this might be ELSIE. (the name of the lady in the case).
The other word in the message was like this ---E.
It seemed it had to be COME
So Holmes had 6 more letters

→C →O →M →L
→S →I

Holmes looked at the first message again. Now it read: -M-ERE --E SL-NE-. The first word must be AM, and the second word was obviously HERE. So that made the last two words A-E SLANE

Holmes cabled New York to see if the police there knew any criminal called ABE SLANEY

Meantime, he looked at message Number 2 again. It now read: A- ELRI-ES. The first word had to be AT. The second word was probably the name of a hotel - perhaps ELRIGES.

husband into her confidence both pointed in that direction. I therefore cabled to my friend, Wilson Hargreave, of the New York Police Bureau, who has more than once made use of my knowledge of London crime. I asked him whether the name of Abe Slaney was known to him. Here is his reply: 'The most dangerous crook in Chicago.' On the very evening upon which I had his answer Hilton Cubitt sent me the last message from Slaney. Working with known letters it took this form:

ELSIE . RE . ARE TO MEET THY GO .

The addition of a P and a D completed a message which showed me that the rascal was proceeding from persuasion to threats, and my knowledge of the crooks of Chicago prepared me to find that he might very rapidly put his words into action. I at once came to Norfolk with my friend and colleague, Dr. Watson, but, unhappily, only in time to find that the worst had already occurred."

When Holmes arrived at the Cubitts' house, it appeared that Elsie had shot her husband, and had then tried to kill herself. If you want to know how Holmes discovered the real murderer you will have to read the whole story*. He set a trap by sending the message below to Abe Slaney, pretending it came from Elsie:

Can you decipher this, now?

*You will find the story in *The Complete Sherlock Holmes Short Stories* (published by John Murray).

Codes are not always for secrets.

Any good shorthand-typist could read this:

It says: 'This is written in shorthand. With a lot of practice you can write in shorthand almost as quickly as you can speak.'

And there is no secret about the Morse code: anyone can learn it. It was made up by an American called Samuel Morse who lived from 1791 to 1872. He started off as a portrait painter; but during a voyage across the Atlantic he got caught up in a conversation about the idea of sending messages over long distances, using the newly invented methods of making electricity. This idea fascinated him: he gave up painting, and for four years he worked on the problem — not just the code, but also how to send the signals.

Other people were also trying to invent ways of doing this, and although Sam Morse's solution was not the only one, it was the most successful. Another idea, which was used for a time by the American railways, is described on pp. 9 and 10.

The Morse code

```
A  ·—          G  ——·        N  —·         U  ··—
B  —···        H  ····        O  ———        V  ···—
C  —·—·        I  ··          P  ·——·       W  ·——
D  —··         J  ·———        Q  ——·—       X  —··—
E  ·           K  —·—         R  ·—·        Y  —·——
F  ··—·        L  ·—··        S  ···        Z  ——··
               M  ——          T  —
```

Here are some questions to think about:

There are two possible signals which use just one bleep:

    (1) One short bleep (E).
    (2) One long bleep (T).

How many possible signals are there which use
    (1) just two bleeps?
    (2) just three bleeps?
    (3) just four bleeps?

Are these all used in the Morse code?

Can you guess (or work out) how many possible signals there would be using just five bleeps?

Another question: Sherlock Holmes listed the letters of the alphabet which are most commonly used in the English language (see p. 4). Does it seem as though Sam Morse took this into account when he made up his code?

Sam Morse used just two kinds of signals — a long bleep and a short bleep. Suppose he had used three kinds. What might they have been? Make up a new code using three kinds of signals. Would it have been better in some ways? Would there be any snags?

The picture on the right shows an instrument for sending messages by telegraph. It was another solution to the problem that Sam Morse spent four years thinking about (see p. 8). But now it's only found in museums.

But you may spot it in use in some of the Westerns you see on TV, because for a time it was used by the American railways.

The pointers in the middle can be clicked over to left or right, and you can probably see how this can be used to pick out each of the letters.

But notice that there are spaces for only twenty letters. What do you think they did about the missing six letters?

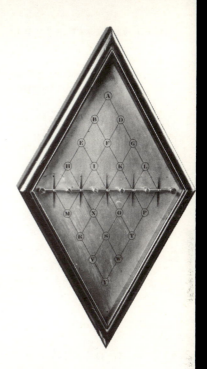

Two of these missing letters occur in the name coded in the diagrams below. If you decode this name you will see what they did for those two letters.

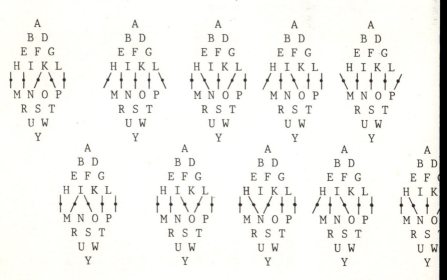

Here is a way of writing down the signals sent by the instrument on p. 9.

o o o o o   means that all five pointers are in their neutral position.

+ o o o o   means that the left-hand pointer has been switched so that its *top* end points to the *right*.

It points to {H, E, B, A} .

o o - o o   means that the middle pointer has been switched so that its *top* end points to the *left*.
It points to {E, I, O, T} .

If these two are done together it gives

+ o - o o   and this means the letter E
i.e. the letter in both {H, E, B, A} and {E, I, O, T} .

```
        A
       B D
      E F G
     H I K L
     M N O P
      R S T
       U W
        Y

        A
       B D
      E F G
     H I K L
     M N O P
      R S T
       U W
        Y
```

Here is a message (read down the columns):

```
o + - o o     + o o - o     o - o + o     o o - o +
o - o + o     + o - o o     + o - o o     + - o o o
              o o - o +     o - + o o     + o o o -
o o - o +     o o - o +     o + o o -     o - + o o
+ - o o o     + o - o o
o + - o o     - o + o o     - + o o o     + o o - o
o - o + o                   + o - o o     - o o o +
              o - o o +     o - o + o
+ o o o -     + o o o -     o - o + o     - + o o o
              - o o o +     + o o o -     o o - + o
                            o o + o -     - o + o o
              o o - o +     + o - o o     o - o + o
              o o - + o     o - o + o     + o - o o
```

What is a binary code?

The Morse code uses just two kinds of signals — a short bleep and a long bleep. Because it uses just two kinds of signal, it is called a *binary* code.

There are quite a lot of binary codes, each invented for a different purpose. Here are the numbers from 0 - 9 coded in four different binary systems.

	0	1	2	3	4	5	6	7	8	9
Morse code	-----	.----	..---	...--	....-	.....	-....	--...	---..	----.
Binary numerals	0	1	10	11	100	101	110	111	1000	1001
Computer tape	(see figure)									
Braille	(see figure)									

The last of these, Braille, is a method of writing that can be used by blind people. It was invented by Louise Braille in 1833.

Each letter is made up of a pattern of raised dots which the reader can feel with his fingers, as you can see in the picture on p. 11. These dots have to be grouped so that the reader can tell which of the dots go together. He must also be able to tell when a dot is missing — a missing dot is just as important as a dot which is there. This is what makes braille a binary code. It is made up of two kinds of signal — a dot and no-dot.

Louise Braille thought up the idea of using a base of six positions arranged in a small rectangle like this:

• •
• •
• •

There are 64 different patterns that can be made from this arrangement. Some of the patterns that are used are shown in the key at the bottom of p. 12. You will see that the letters in the top row (A-J) use just the top four of the six possible places. (Can you find some patterns, using those four places, which are not included in that top row of letters?)
Look also at the way the rows 2, 3, and 5, are related to the top row.

Using the key below, see if you can decipher the piece of poetry above.

Making things more difficult for the code breakers.

All the codes in this book so far have been plain codes. In a plain code each letter is always mapped on to the same symbol

For example:　　A　　C　　(Codex)
　　　　　or　　A　　.—　　(Morse)
　　　　　or　　A　　🯅　　(Dancing men)

For people like Sherlock Holmes, a plain code is not too difficult to crack. But his method would not work for a code in which A sometimes became C, and sometimes became Y, and sometimes V, all in the same message.

This would not be a plain code. We'll call it a *scrambled* code.

Using the codex to make a scrambled code.

The codex really makes six different codes (see p. 1). So to make a scrambled code you could just keep jumping from one of these codes to another.

But there is a snag: how will the person you're sending the message to know when you are making a jump — and which code you're jumping to?

Here is one way out: first you agree to jump codes at the beginning of each new sentence. Then, to tell him which code to use next, you've got to tell him how to decode one letter. He will then be able to set his inner hexagon to the right position. So you agree that you will put a pair of letters at the beginning of each sentence. To someone not in the secret, this will look just like a two-letter word, but really you will be saying which code is going to be used in that sentence.

For instance, **kf** at the beginning of a sentence would mean: Turn the inner hexagon so that **k** (on the inside) is opposite **f** (on the outside).

A codex scrambled message.

Kf xpye ye a ebdgbx qbeeawb. Rc wbg ieh pywepy vs? Rb flcul sgwwgb nuupbo hnow newga ca wlg unrgr hgoovxg? Wk khaxh af iofm tycpqcbm ab mhc lcxolcl icffsc? Lx nvcq y lvnnyuv xgev drgn dt ptia kagvcq.

If you decoded the message on p. 13, the answer to the first question is certainly 'Yes'. The answers to the second and third questions are 'G' and 'E'.

How often do the other letters crop up? Compare these letter frequencies in the coded message with those in the decoded one. And then compare these with Sherlock Holmes' ideas about the most frequently used letters (see p. 4) Do you think he was right about this?

A square scramble

Another way of making a scrambled code uses a key like this square of letters on the right:

Q	A	W	S	X
E	D	C	R	F
V	T	G	B	Y
H	N	U	M	J
I	K	O	L	P

This key is made by putting the first 25 letters of the alphabet in a square. The order does not matter. The letters are jumbled up anyhow. There's no room for Z, so we put Z = S in coding.

Here is how the coding is done:

(1) Write out the message: Meet at midnight
(2) Code the letters in pairs; the first pair is: m, e
(3) Find this pair in the key. The letters are at the corners of a rectangle.

E . . .
. . . .
. . . M

(4) Find the letters at the other corners: R and H

So me is coded as **rh**

(Note: you might have read the code as **hr**. You have to agree at the start which way round to read off from the square. Here the code letter will be taken from the same *column* as the letter being coded.)
So 'Meet at midnight' is coded as **'Rhvd ta lhndvovn'**.

You can see that this is pretty well scrambled: m is first r and then l, and the letter v occurs three times in the coded message. The first time it means 'e', then it means 'i', and then 'h'. But there are still some problems to sort out with your partner before you start using this code: how will you code oc?   li?   oo?
What will you do with the last letter of a message with an odd number of letters?

luu snaf tepefertn rittrer wna v rceuli et nihr wckhkg?

A looking glass scramble

Another way of making a scrambled code was suggested by Lewis Carroll, using the letter square below:

	A B C D E F G H I J K L M N O P Q R S T U V W X Y Z	
A	a b c d e f g h i j k l m n o p q r s t u v w x y z	A
B	b c d e f g h i j k l m n o p q r s t u v w x y z a	B
C	c d e f g h i j k l m n o p q r s t u v w x y z a b	C
D	d e f g h i j k l m n o p q r s t u v w x y z a b c	D
E	e f g h i j k l m n o p q r s t u v w x y z a b c d	E
F	f g h i j k l m n o p q r s t u v w x y z a b c d e	F
G	g h i j k l m n o p q r s t u v w x y z a b c d e f	G
H	h i j k l m n o p q r s t u v w x y z a b c d e f g	H
I	i j k l m n o p q r s t u v w x y z a b c d e f g h	I
J	j k l m n o p q r s t u v w x y z a b c d e f g h i	J
K	k l m n o p q r s t u v w x y z a b c d e f g h i j	K
L	l m n o p q r s t u v w x y z a b c d e f g h i j k	L
M	m n o p q r s t u v w x y z a b c d e f g h i j k l	M
N	n o p q r s t u v w x y z a b c d e f g h i j k l m	N
O	o p q r s t u v w x y z a b c d e f g h i j k l m n	O
P	p q r s t u v w x y z a b c d e f g h i j k l m n o	P
Q	q r s t u v w x y z a b c d e f g h i j k l m n o p	Q
R	r s t u v w x y z a b c d e f g h i j k l m n o p q	R
S	s t u v w x y z a b c d e f g h i j k l m n o p q r	S
T	t u v w x y z a b c d e f g h i j k l m n o p q r s	T
U	u v w x y z a b c d e f g h i j k l m n o p q r s t	U
V	v w x y z a b c d e f g h i j k l m n o p q r s t u	V
W	w x y z a b c d e f g h i j k l m n o p q r s t u v	W
X	x y z a b c d e f g h i j k l m n o p q r s t u v w	X
Y	y z a b c d e f g h i j k l m n o p q r s t u v w x	Y
Z	z a b c d e f g h i j k l m n o p q r s t u v w x y	Z
	A B C D E F G H I J K L M N O P Q R S T U V W X Y Z	

With this square you can map any letter-pair onto a single letter.
    For instance: (C, H) → j
(Find C and H in the outside alphabets: the C-row and the H-column meet at j).

Now choose any word you like for a key word. We'll have WONDERLAND.

Write out your message: S E E Y O U A T S L O O P Y'S
Write the key word underneath (repeating it W O N D E R L A N D W O N D
if necessary):   ↓ ↓ ↓ ↓ ↓ ↓ ↓ ↓ ↓ ↓ ↓ ↓ ↓ ↓
Use the letter-square to code: o s r b s l l t f o k c c b'

By using the letter-square inside out you can decode a message — but only if you know the key word. Try it on this (key word: ALICE):

lpekw clztslw etstp 'Inmcp qp Aoylgvllvf'.

AN ANAGRAM CODE

An anagram of a word is made by shuffling its letters. This disguises the word, so it can be used as a kind of code. But a code has to be decoded by someone, so you have to have some rule for shuffling the letters.

The rule described below uses *uni-composite numbers*. You won't know what these are because 'uni-composite' is a made-up word! So first read the note at the bottom of page 2.

Here is the coding method:
The letters of each *sentence* are shuffled separately.
First, count the number of letters in the sentence you are coding.
    If the number is uni-composite — fine.
    If not, make it up to the next uni-composite number by adding X's at the end.
    For example: CAN YOU LEND ME TEN P?
        16 letters. Not uni-composite. The next uni-composite number is 21 — so add 5 X's.
        CANYOULENDMETENPXXXXX?

The next step is to arrange these letters in a rectangle.
In this case there are 21 letters, and 21 = 3 x 7. So the rectangle will have 3 rows, with 7 letters in each row. (We agree to count the bigger number across the page).

        C A N Y O U L
        E N D M E T E
        N P X X X X X

The message you send is made by reading down the columns. You can group the letters in threes, or disguise them even more like this:

        CENAN PND XY MXOE XUT X LEX?

To decode this you have to do everything backwards. See how it works with this message, and then try decoding the two sentences below. (Remember you deal with each sentence separately).
TDE HOBE FOET ONHK! NAOO EOI OVFWCY EWE WRRONY LAI EUDOO YTTR SUTS ESF X HSTS TRX.